DISNEY · PIXAR

COCO

TOP 10s
THE POWER OF MUSIC

JENNIFER BOOTHROYD

LERNER PUBLICATIONS ◆ MINNEAPOLIS

Lerner Publications Company
A division of Lerner Publishing Group, Inc.
241 First Avenue North
Minneapolis, MN 55401 USA

For reading levels and more information, look up this title at www.lernerbooks.com.

Main body text set in ITC Avant Garde Gothic 13/14.
Typeface provided by International Typeface Corp.

Library of Congress Cataloging-in-Publication Data

Names: Boothroyd, Jennifer, 1972– author.
Title: Coco top 10s : the power of music / Jennifer Boothroyd.
Other titles: Coco top tens
Description: Minneapolis : Lerner Publications, 2019. | Series: My top 10 disney | Includes bibliographical references. | Audience: Age 6–10. | Audience: K to Grade 3.
Identifiers: LCCN 2018015742 (print) | LCCN 2018034057 (ebook) | ISBN 9781541543591 (eb pdf) | ISBN 9781541539105 (lb : alk. paper)
Subjects: LCSH: Coco (Motion picture)—Juvenile literature.
Classification: LCC PN1997.2.C62 (ebook) | LCC PN1997.2.C62 B66 20109 (print) | DDC 791.43/72—dc23

LC record available at https://lccn.loc.gov/2018015742

Manufactured in the United States of America
1-45093-35920-7/17/2018

TABLE OF CONTENTS

WHAT MAKES *COCO* GREAT?

WHAT COMES TO MIND WHEN YOU THINK ABOUT THE MOVIE *COCO*? Is it the fun characters? The music? The fantastic places? There are many things to love about *Coco*. This book lists some of those fabulous things! But these lists are opinions. And unlike facts, opinions might change from person to person. Do you feel the same way, or do you have different ideas? There are no right or wrong answers when you share your opinions.

SO COME ALONG ON A JOURNEY INTO THE WORLD OF *COCO* AND DECIDE YOUR FAVORITES!

TOP 10 PLACES IN *COCO* WE WANT TO VISIT

10 Santa Cecilia

THERE'S SO MUCH TO EXPLORE IN THE TOWN.

9 The Sunrise Spectacular stadium

8 The tallest building in the Land of the Dead

THE VIEW WOULD BE BREATHTAKING.

7 Plaza de la Cruz

6 Mariachi Plaza

HOW COOL WOULD IT BE TO HEAR ALL THOSE MUSICIANS PERFORM?

5 Rivera family courtyard

4 Marigold Grand Central Station

3 Santa Cecilia Cemetery

2 The Marigold Bridge

THERE MUST BE A MILLION PETALS!

1

« DE LA CRUZ'S MANSION

THERE'S A POOL SHAPED LIKE A GUITAR!

TOP 10 TIMES MIGUEL SPOKE FROM THE HEART

10 "This isn't a dream then. You're all really out there."

TO HIS DEAD ANCESTORS

9 "These aren't just old pictures. They're our family, and they're counting on us to remember them."

MIGUEL IS TEACHING HIS BABY SISTER THE IMPORTANCE OF THE OFRENDA.

8 "My whole life, there's been something that made me different . . . now I know it comes from you."

TO HÉCTOR

7 "I've gotta seize my moment."

6 "Your Papá, he wanted you to have this."

DON'T FORGET HIM, MAMÁ COCO!

^ ^ ^ ^ ^

DID YOU KNOW?

Anthony Gonzalez was ten years old when he started working as the voice of Miguel. He was thirteen when the movie was finished.

5 "This isn't fair—it's my life! You already had yours."

TO MAMÁ IMELDA

4 "You don't have to forgive him, but we shouldn't forget him!"

ASKING MAMÁ IMELDA TO HELP HÉCTOR

3 "You should be the one the world remembers, not de la Cruz!"

TO HÉCTOR

2 "I don't just want to get de la Cruz's blessing. I need to prove that . . . that I'm worthy of it."

1

"FAMILY COMES FIRST."

9

TOP 10 REASONS DANTE IS TERRIFIC

10 His version of shake is adorable!
NOT JUST HIS PAW, HIS WHOLE BODY!

9 His tongue is so floppy.

8 He knows how to climb trees.

7 His tiny spirit guide wings are too cute.

6 He finds Miguel and Héctor in the pit.

5

He tries very hard to save Miguel from falling.

4   He tries to bring Miguel back to Héctor.

HE KNOWS MIGUEL'S TRUE PATH.

3   He is so   happy rolling in the petals on the Marigold Bridge.

2

He's loyal and persistent.

1

HE BECOMES AN ALEBRIJE.

FRIDA WAS RIGHT! HE IS A SPIRIT GUIDE.

TOP 10 RIVERA FAMILY'S DÍA DE LOS MUERTOS TRADITIONS

10 Abuelita decorates the ofrenda room with lots and lots of beautiful orange marigolds.

9 Candles light the way in the dark.

8 The family decorates with colorful sugar skulls.

THE SKULLS ARE BEAUTIFUL AND MEANINGFUL.

7 They share stories of their ancestors

6 The family spends time together.

5 They enjoy favorite family foods.

ABUELITA'S COOKING LOOKS YUMMY!

4 The children help make a path of petals to guide their ancestors home.

3 The family makes music together.

THAT'S A NEW TRADITION!

2 Papel picado decorates the courtyard.

THE CUT-PAPER PICTURES LOOK SO DELICATE.

1

THEY MAKE AN OFRENDA TO REMEMBER THEIR LOVED ONES.

⇐

TOP 10 TIMES *COCO* TOUCHED OUR HEARTS

 **10** Héctor's picture sinks under the water.

HOW WILL HE BE ON THE OFRENDA?

 **9**

Héctor, Mamá Imelda, and Mamá Coco cross the Marigold Bridge together.

 **8** Miguel shows his baby sister the ofrenda.

7 Mamá Imelda changes her mind about Miguel playing music.

6 Abuelita breaks Miguel's guitar.

AND OUR HEARTS TOO.

5 Héctor talks about missing his little girl.

4 Chicharrón disappears in the final death.

3 Miguel tells Mamá Coco pretty much everything.

LOVE THE WRESTLING MASKS!

2 Miguel and his cousins play music in the family courtyard.

1

MAMÁ COCO'S PICTURE IS ON THE OFRENDA.

SHE WILL BE MISSED AND REMEMBERED.

TOP 10 FAVORITE MUSICAL MOMENTS IN *COCO*

10 Ernesto de la Cruz's final performance in the Land of the Living.

TOO BAD ABOUT THAT BELL.

9 Miguel sings at the party to get Ernesto's attention.

8 Héctor plays Chicharrón's favorite song.

7 Mamá Imelda sings in the Sunrise Spectacular.

6 Héctor helps Miguel develop his grito, or loud musical yell.

5

Miguel and the whole family sing together.

4

Miguel suggests some music to add to Frida's performance.

HE'S A COMPOSER *AND* A MUSICIAN.

3

Miguel practices his guitar in his hideout.

2

The bands compete in Plaza de la Cruz.

SO MANY INCREDIBLE PERFORMANCES!

1

MIGUEL AND MAMÁ COCO SING "REMEMBER ME."

17

QUIZ BREAK!

Are you a *Coco* expert?
Take this quiz and find out!

1

WHERE DO PEOPLE IN THE LAND OF THE DEAD GO WHEN THEY HAVE TROUBLE CROSSING THE BRIDGE?

A Department of Family Reunions
B Family Fun Department
C Department of Ofrendas
D Problem Department

2

WHAT IS THE SHAPE OF ERNESTO'S POOL?

A a guitar
B a skull
C an oval
D a music note

3

WHAT IS MIGUEL'S SHOE SIZE?

A 8.5
B 8
C 7.5
D 7

WHICH OF THESE THINGS IS SHAPED LIKE A SKULL IN THE LAND OF THE DEAD?

A a pay phone
B a skull scanner panel
C De la Cruz's fireworks
D all of the above

4

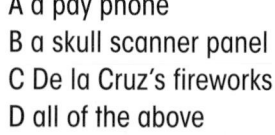

5

IN REAL LIFE, FRIDA KAHLO IS A FAMOUS _____?

A actress
B singer
C painter
D chef

6

WHO HAS A PICTURE OF JUAN ORTODONCIA ON THE OFRENDA?

A his teacher
B his dentist
C his best friend
D his neighbor

7

WHERE CAN YOU SEE BUZZ AND WOODY IN *COCO*?

A in a piñata stand
B in an alebrije stand
C on a poster in Mariachi Plaza
D on a sugar skull stand

8

MAMÁ IMELDA IS MIGUEL'S _____?

A mother
B grandmother
C great-grandmother
D great-great-grandmother

9

WHAT DOES "UN POCO LOCO" MEAN?

A a poky train
B a little crazy
C a prime location
D a lost pocket

10

WHICH SPIRIT GUIDE HAS A FROG BODY AND RABBIT EARS?

A hoppy
B ribbit
C rabbog
D frobbit

TOP 10 FUNNIEST LINES FROM *COCO*

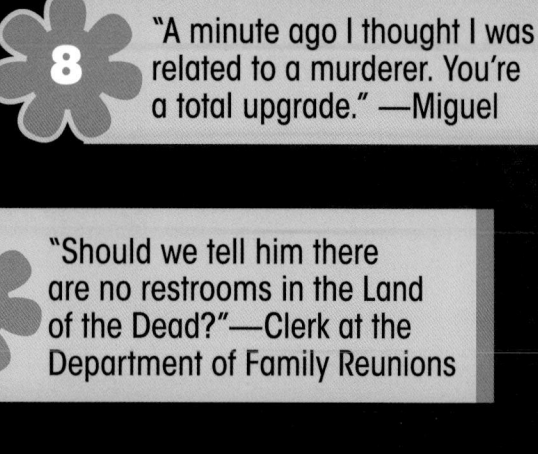

10 "Watch your step, they make caquitas everywhere."

TÍO FELIPE DOESN'T WANT DIRTY SHOES!

9 "Never name a street dog. They'll follow you forever."

ABUELITA DOESN'T KNOW THAT DANTE ALREADY FOLLOWS MIGUEL EVERYWHERE.

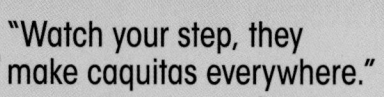

8 "A minute ago I thought I was related to a murderer. You're a total upgrade." —Miguel

7 "Should we tell him there are no restrooms in the Land of the Dead?"—Clerk at the Department of Family Reunions

6 "I'm one Frida short of an opening number."

CECI IS MAD HÉCTOR LOST THE COSTUME.

5 "Ernesto doesn't *do* rehearsals." —Frida

4 "I hope you die very soon—you know what I mean." —Ernesto

3 "I thought it might've been one of those made-up things that adults tell kids, like vitamins." —Miguel

2 "Stop pestering the celebrities." —Héctor

1 "THAT DEVIL BOX TELLS YOU NOTHING BUT LIES."

MAMÁ IMELDA DOESN'T TRUST COMPUTERS.

TOP 10 FAVORITE FOODS IN *COCO*

10 Mole.

9 Chorizo.

A SPICY SAUSAGE AND HÉCTOR'S NICKNAME.

8 Pan de muertos.

MANY FAMILIES SPEND THE WEEK LEADING UP TO DÍA DE LOS MUERTOS MAKING THIS BREAD.

7 Papaya.

IT'S A *HUGE* PART OF FRIDA'S PERFORMANCE.

6 Churros.

DID YOU KNOW?

Sugar skulls are decorations made from sugar. Originally, the Aztecs who lived in the area that is modern-day Mexico made these sweets from seeds and honey. Today some are fully edible and some are not.

5 Elotes.

YUMMY CORN IN A CHILI-AND-LIME SAUCE WITH CHEESE!

4 Pan dulce.

A TASTY SWEET BREAD.

3 Tamales.

ALWAYS ACCEPT MORE TAMALES FROM ABUELITA.

2 Taquitos.

A PORCUPINE ALEBRIJE MAKES A GREAT SNACK HOLDER.

1

SUGAR SKULLS.

TOP 10 REASONS MIGUEL'S HIDEOUT IS AWESOME

10 The rug makes it cozy.

9 There is a fan to keep it cool.

8 He can listen to his favorite songs on a record player.

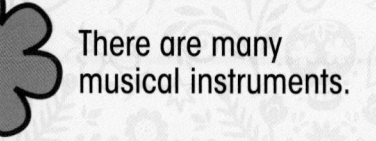

PERFECT FOR A YOUNG MUSICIAN!

7 There are many musical instruments.

6 It has cool mood lighting.

LOTS OF CANDLES!

5 There's a secret entrance.

4

He can watch the best of Ernesto de la Cruz on videotape.

HE'S MEMORIZED ALL OF ERNESTO'S LINES.

When one of *Coco*'s animators was a child, he would watch old clips of Disney animators to learn more about drawing. This inspired the idea for how Miguel learns to play guitar.

3 Dante and Miguel have a place to hang out together.

2 It's a special place for Miguel's treasures and collectibles.

HE HAS QUITE THE COLLECTION!

1

MIGUEL CAN PRACTICE PLAYING HIS GUITAR.

HE'S PROBABLY SPENT HOURS AND HOURS HERE.

TOP 10 JAW-DROPPING MOMENTS IN *COCO*

10 When Abuelita throws her sandal.

SHE MEANS BUSINESS.

9 Seeing the Día de los Muertos party at Ernesto de la Cruz's mansion.

8 When Héctor plays the guitar for Chicharrón.

HE'S SO TALENTED!

7 When Miguel becomes invisible to the living.

6 When Miguel and Héctor realize they are family.

5 Miguel discovers the guitar in Mamá Coco's picture.

4 Whenever Pepita does anything. SHE'S INCREDIBLE.

3 When Héctor realizes that Ernesto poisoned him.

2 The first time Miguel sees the Marigold Bridge and the Land of the Dead.

1 WHEN MIGUEL STRUMS THE GUITAR IN ERNESTO'S TOMB.

WOW! WHAT A MOMENT.

TOP 10 REASONS ALEBRIJES ARE FANTASTIC

10 They are magical works of art.

9 They look ordinary in the Land of the Living.

8 Some are good trackers.

PEPITA MADE MIGUEL'S FOOTSTEPS GLOW.

7 They are loyal.

6 Some breathe fire.

5 They glow in the dark.

BEST NIGHT-LIGHT EVER!

4 They travel between the Land of the Living and the Land of the Dead.

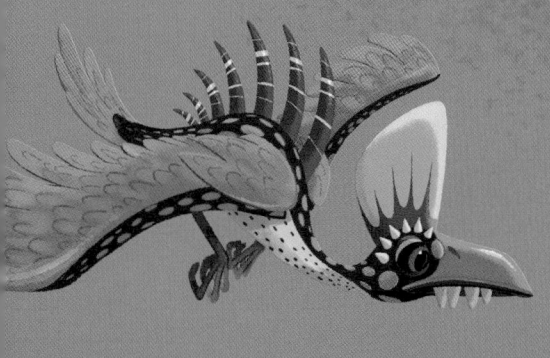

3 They can be a mix of different animals and creatures.

LIKE THE FROBBIT!

2 They help people find their path.

1 THEY ARE COLORFUL.

VERY, VERY COLORFUL!

MAKE YOUR OWN
COCO TOP 10!

OUR JOURNEY THROUGH *COCO* MAY BE OVER, BUT THE STORY DOESN'T HAVE TO END HERE. Copy the blank list on the next page. Do you have a different opinion about one of the lists in this book? Change it up!

DO YOU HAVE FAVORITE COSTUMES OR FAVORITE SONGS FROM THE MOVIE?

WHAT WOULD BE THE BEST PARTS OF HAVING A SPIRIT ANIMAL?

HOW DOES *COCO* INSPIRE YOU?

Now is the time to seize your moment and make your own top ten list!

COPY THIS PAGE!

MY

Disney · PIXAR
COCO

TOP 10:

10. _____

9. _____

8. _____

7. _____

6. _____

5. _____

4. _____

3. _____

2. _____

1. _____

TO LEARN MORE

Books

Dakin, Glenn. Coco: *The Essential Guide.* New York: DK, 2017.
This guide will help you become an expert on the world of *Coco.*
Discover fantastic facts and interesting details about Miguel and his
extended family.

Murray, Julie. *Day of the Dead.* Edina, MN: Abdo, 2014.
Covering everything from the history of Día de los Muertos to
traditions and symbols of the festivities, this book will help you
learn all about the holiday that inspired *Coco*!

Websites

National Geographic Kids: Day of the Dead
https://kids.nationalgeographic.com/explore/celebrations/day-of
-the-dead/
Learn about the many ways the Day of the Dead holiday is
celebrated.

Pixar: *Coco*
https://www.pixar.com/feature-films/coco#coco-main
Learn more about the creation of the film *Coco* from
the people who made it. Watch trailers and view
concept art.